The GIFT of POETRY

The GIFT of POETRY

Alice Hack

Pleasant Word
A Division of WINEPRESS PUBLISHING

Printed in the United States of America

Packaged by Pleasant Word, a division of WinePress Publishing, PO Box 428, Enumclaw, WA 98022. The views expressed or implied in this work do not necessarily reflect those of Pleasant Word, a division of WinePress Publishing. Ultimate design, content, and editorial accuracy of this work are the responsibilities of the author.

Unless otherwise noted, Scripture quotations in this book are taken from the King James Version of the Bible.

ISBN 1-57921-531-9
Library of Congress Catalog Card Number: 2002115816

Table of Contents

Blessed Abundantly

I've been blessed abundantly
Much more than words can say.
Blessed with five lovely children
To brighten up my day.

Just why you placed them in my care,
Lord, I do not know.
I've been blessed abundantly
Just watching as they grow.

I've seen them laugh with joy
I've wiped away their tears.
With a gentle word of love
I've chased away their fears.

Lord, if they should catch a glimpse
Of You somewhere in me,
Then my life has surely been
Blessed so abundantly.

Big or Small

When I was just a little girl
I prayed upon my knees,
Asking God if He would
Give me a sister, please.

I will take good care of her,
I will love her so.
I know that I am little,
But together we can grow.

One day my mother said, "My dear,
I have some news for you.
I'm going to have a baby
Soon it will be due."

Finally the day arrived
My heart was in a whirl.
When Daddy smiling said to me,
"Mom had a baby girl."

Makes no difference big or small
One thing I learned that day.
A merciful and loving God
Hears us when we pray.

Beneath a Smile

She always wears a lovely smile
Giggles in a silly way.
One glance at her and you would think
That all went well that day.

She doesn't dare let others know
The burdens that she bears.
Although a smile is on her face
Her world is full of cares.

Criticized for the things she does,
For the things she doesn't do.
Smiling whatever may come,
Keeping God's grace in view.

Sometimes I sense beneath that smile
The pain she doesn't share.
That's when God's Spirit whispers,
The Pastor's wife needs prayer.

Before the Break of Day

You awoke me with a nudge
I heard you gently say,
Let's meet together, child,
Before the break of day.

I tossed and turned upon my bed
I'm too tired now to pray.
But the Lord kept nudging me
Before the break of day.

My flesh said, Go back to sleep
In bed I want to stay.
But the Spirit gently woke me up
Before the break of day.

In the early morning hours
The Spirit had His way,
We shared in sweet fellowship
Before the break of day.

Be Still

Be still and know that I am God,
Don't grumble and complain.
With the Word of truth be shod,
For in My Word there's gain.

Be still, my little child so weak,
By faith just trust in me.
If My will you daily seek,
New heights you soon will see.

Be still and let Me lead the way,
Hold onto My hand.
Pray and read My Word each day
Follow my commands.

Be still, little child of Mine,
Trust in My Word so true.
Love Me with all your heart,
Until I come for you.

Along Life's Way

All things work together for good
To those who know the Lord,
It is written in God's Word
Our breastplate and our sword.

Temptations will surround us
Trials knock upon our door.
With the helmet of Salvation
We'll be safe forever more.

The road will not be easy
Darkness will dim our eyes.
Faith will be our shield
Beneath those cloudy skies.

The joy of the Lord will be our strength
Throughout each day.
So we have no need to fear
As we go along life's way.

A Still Small Voice

I'm listening for God's still small voice
I know that soon He'll speak.
He will tell me what to do
As His will I seek.

God speaks to me in different ways,
Sometimes it's through His word.
Sometimes as I kneel in prayer
God's still small voice is heard.

Then sometimes it's through a friend
He has sent into my life.
Sometimes He speaks to me
Through heartaches, pain, and strife.

In whatever way He chooses
In God I will rejoice.
For each day I long to hear
My Savior's still small voice.

A Sponge

As I held a sponge within my hand
These thoughts entered my mind,
Lord, may I become just like this sponge
As our hearts entwine.

Saturate me with your love,
As in you I abide.
Fill me with your holiness
That in You I might hide.

May I absorb the faith
That You so freely give,
That others see You in me
As on this earth I live.

When this sponge is finally filled,
Lord, then I will know
That through this earthen vessel
Your love will surely flow.

Broken Vessel

A vessel was shaped
By the Potter's hand.
This fine piece of clay
Was placed on a stand.

So pleased was the Potter
He thought in his mind,
This vessel of beauty
Is one of a kind

Designed to be used
In a special way.
When suddenly an upset
Broke this piece of clay.

God picked up the pieces
Reshaped it again.
Now this vessel is better
Than it's ever been.

God's Vessel

Just a vessel in Your hands
Lord, mold me as You may.
Let my life bring glory
To Your name today.

This vessel through the years
You've had to reshape now and then.
Although this vessel let You down
On You it could depend.

This vessel the world without doubt
Would have quickly cast away.
But with Your tender mercies, Lord,
You reshaped this piece of clay.

Reshaped this vessel with Your love
Gave it a brand new start.
Out of this piece of worn out clay
You've made a piece of art.

God's Sovereignty

God created in six days
The world and its fullness.
The wonders of His ways
Fill my heart with blissfulness.

As I look at His creation
The beauty that I see.
Makes me bow in adoration
To the God of Calvary.

He is a God of divine power
We should never cause Him shame.
For He is a mighty tower
He knows us each by name.

God who came to earth
In the form of Jesus Christ.
To Him our soul was worth
This pearl of great price.

So let us daily sing
Of this God of Calvary.
Our Savior and our King
Who died to set us free.

God's Blessing

When God is about to bless me
It is very plain to see,
Satan tries his hardest
To get the best of me.

He fills me with discouragement
Places doubts within my heart.
Then I know quite well
God's blessing soon will start.

Satan gets quite angry
You should see him throw a fit.
But it does not stop God's blessing,
Not one single bit.

So when I feel down-hearted
I bow my head and pray.
Thank You, Lord, for the blessing
You're about to send my way.

Go and Tell

Today, my child, you must tell
Someone of my love
So they too can dwell
In Heaven's home above.

Today, my child, is the day
For souls to be set free.
Tell them that I'm the way
For I'm the door, you see.

Today, my child, pray
For souls outside my fold.
Child, please don't delay
For many must be told.

Go tell that Jesus is the one
He died upon the cross.
God sent his only son
To redeem the lost.

Go tell that Christ arose again,
In Heaven He now reigns.
Christ bore the marks of sin
So Heaven we can gain.

Fruit

A tree is known
By the fruit it bears.
Apple trees cannot grow
Big yellow pears.

These fruits of the Spirit
Will abide in the heart,
Love joy, peace and temperance
And that's just a start.

Longsuffering, gentleness and goodness
Should also abound.
If Christ is your vine
These fruits will be found.

Don't forget faith and meekness
Nine fruits in all.
A fruit from its tree,
Won't very far fall.

From Within

The Lord changes from the inside
Not from the outside in.
Search for Him with all your heart
He will cleanse away your sin.

He will change your way of thinking
As He works from deep within.
The heart is truly wicked,
So it's there He must begin.

Man can change the outside
While traveling life's highway.
By doing deeds of kindness
Good works throughout each day.

God's Spirit must reside
Before the change begins.
The change cannot take place
From the outside in.

I Forgot to Pray

I've blamed You, Lord, much too long,
When troubles came my way.
It seems when everything went wrong,
I just forgot to pray.

I've blamed You, Lord, and turned my back
On you and went astray.
Of your power I lost track,
When I forgot to pray.

I've blamed You, Lord, for each mistake
That I've made every day.
On myself I've brought heartache
When I forgot to pray.

I've blamed You, Lord, can you forgive?
By my side please stay.
Teach me again for you to live
And once again to pray.

Forbidden Prayer

I remember as a child
Teacher would softly say,
Children, please bow your heads
It is time to pray,

She would ask the Lord for wisdom
To teach those placed in her care.
It was just a natural thing to do,
Begin the day with prayer.

Now in schools across our land
Prayers dare not be said.
Since this law has passed
We see drugs and guns instead.

Teachers no longer in control
What a price we pay.
Children's lives put on the line
In school rooms every day.

Destruction in the schools
Across the U.S.A.
Because before each class begins
Teachers cannot pray.

Fellowship

Today my sister hurt me
She was so very cruel,
I must admit I'm angry
But anger is Satan's tool.

Lord, give to me Your wisdom,
Show me what I must do.
My Flesh would like to see
My sister hurting too.

The Human side of me
Vengeance is sure to seek,
I know the Spirit's willing
But the flesh is very weak.

God gently whispered to me,
"Forgiveness is the way.
Don't let those seeds of anger
Lead our fellowship astray."

Faith

Faith in Christ Jesus
When your way is not clear.
Faith will move mountains
As doubts disappear.

Faith is the substance
Of things hoped for.
Faith is the key
That unlocks Heaven's door.

Faith will in a moment
Move God's mighty hand.
God always blesses
When faith leads a man.

The impossible happens
As I very well know.
All things are possible
When faith has control.

Faith Isn't Just a Word

I know a man who walks by faith
God's love through him is shown.
My faith has grown stronger
Because this man I've known.

I know the burden that he bears
Is more than I could stand.
I've yet to hear this man complain
I don't think that he can.

I've only heard him thank the Lord
For all that He has done
He says God blesses him each day
From dawn till setting sun.

Faith isn't just a word to him
He walks by faith each day.
I'm blessed because the Lord allowed
This man to pass my way.

Enjoy the Ride

Just sit back, enjoy the ride
The Lord is in control.
He sees the danger up ahead
Your safety is His goal.

Just sit back, enjoy the ride
Let Jesus lead the way.
The armor God has given you
Will see you through each day.

The obstacles in your path
Are in God's perfect view.
Sit right back, enjoy life's ride
He's watching over you.

So sit back, enjoy the ride
The Lord has paid the fee
It won't be long when we arrive
Heaven is our destiny.

Energizer

Have you ever heard of the energizer,
The battery that keeps going and going?
I know a woman who loves the Lord
That keeps sowing and sowing.

Sowing seeds of kindness
Tired but smiling still,
Loving the Lord with her whole heart
Quietly doing His will.

I watch her sow seeds of kindness
Not letting pettiness get in her way,
Faithfully laboring for the Lord
Pleasing Him everyday.

I tease her cause I know I can,
Calling her by the battery's name.
The energizer keeps going, I say
But this woman puts me to shame.

Like water runs off a duck's back
Cruel words don't faze her one bit.
Satan, you may as well give up the fight
This woman will never quit.

Don't Dwell

Don't dwell, my friend, upon the past
Those things you've said and done,
Those failures made along life's way
Don't count them one by one.

Do dwell upon the blessings
God has given you today.
The sweetness of His fellowship
When you kneel and pray.

Count the joy of sharing
The faith that you hold fast,
Those who accomplish much for God
Do not dwell on the past.

Christ has washed away your sins
Cast them in the deepest sea.
Forgotten and forgiven them
Why can't you let them be.

Donor

While living in this world
I have a place to stay.
It's called the house I live in
My home of dust and clay.

It's furnished with the things I need
This house in which I dwell.
But when my life is o'er
It's just an empty shell.

I'll be leaving it behind
No use it'll be to me.
If there is anything you need
Take it on your journey.

The world calls me a donor,
But the least that I can do
Is to share God's richest blessing
By giving life to you.

Do Others See Jesus in You?

I went to church last Sunday
Sat down in my favorite pew.
The Preacher spoke on the subject
Do others see Jesus in you?

He told us our life was a mirror
For those all around to see through.
Those words pierced my heart that morning
Do others see Jesus in you?

The tears slowly slid down my cheeks
In my heart I very well knew.
There were times in my life every day
That Jesus was nowhere in view.

He said the words sometimes uttered
Yes, our attitudes too,
Will often hinder others
From seeing Jesus in you.

God spoke to my heart that morning
My life wasn't what it should be.
I prayed God remove all that hinders
That Jesus is seen in me.

Christian Brother

I watched my Christian Brother
Watched him walk from day to day.
If only I could be like him,
As I walk along life's way.

I watched him very closely,
Thought he could do no wrong.
In my eyes this Christian Brother
Was so spiritual and strong.

When the church would meet together
I knew I would find him there.
Always more than willing
To lead us all in prayer.

One day while I was watching him
Quite to my surprise.
This Christian Brother stumbled
Right before my eyes.

I quickly grasped my Savior's hand
Lest I should stumble too.
Thank you, Lord, for teaching me
To keep my eyes on you.

Child, I Care

One day my heart was troubled
I was in deep despair.
As tear drops filled my eyes
A voice whispered, child, I care.

I've brought you this far, child
I am in all ways fair.
Don't feel so down hearted
Child, for you I care.

Don't let this trial get you down
Let's communicate in prayer.
I am God your Savior
Child, for you I care.

By faith just trust in me
This heartache let me share,
Remembering all my promises
You see, my child, I care.

Chastening

If it were not for God's chastening
Where would I be today?
Lord, I would not listen,
To what you had to say.

You saw a critical spirit
Was leading me astray.
Lord, you tried to warn me
But I just went my way.

I was headed for trouble
Puffed up like a big balloon,
You tried, I just wouldn't listen,
So you quickly changed my tune.

Amid the trial you sent me
You whittled me down to size.
I soon learned to pray for my brother
Instead of criticize.

By God's Grace

Our Nation's been disrupted
By an evil plan.
America by God's grace
In unity now stands.

Freedom rings across this land
Old Glory flying high.
Heartbroken over loved ones lost
In unity we cry.

The enemy will not prevail
Not man but God they fight.
A Nation founded on God's Word
Will see all wrongs made right.

The enemy's made one mistake
Woke up a sleeping bear,
A Nation coming back to God
Upon their knees in prayer.

New Beginnings

As I gaze out of the window
New beginnings I see.
New leaves are appearing
On all the oak trees.

I see new grass peeking
Above the ground.
New beginnings are happening
Just look around.

Beginnings of new life
A crispy new start.
New beginnings can also
Start in one's heart.

By faith trust in Jesus
New life will begin.
When you open your heart's door
And let Jesus in.

Never Once Doubted

If your mother could write you from Heaven
With these words she would comfort you.
My son, I never once doubted
You did the best you could do.

I know you thought of me often
I never once doubted your love for me.
Don't bear the pain of a burden
My son, that is so needlessly.

Those times you wrote me a letter
And the presents you sent my way.
It was those times, my son,
Your thoughtfulness brightened my day.

Don't dwell on the things of the past
The things left unsaid and undone.
Just dwell on those special moments
We spent together, my son.

I Know My Savior's Near

I gazed into the sky one day,
I saw a cloud so fair,
Before I knew just what to do
I saw my Savior there.

Then the cloud did disappear
A storm began to roar.
How my heart did fear
As I started for the door.

As I gazed again on high
The cloud appeared so warm,
My Savior stood close by
To still the terrible storm.

Was just a dream I had at night,
As I lay in bed asleep.
But what a glorious blessed light
That dream began to reap.

Now I know within my heart
That Christ my Savior's near.
And naught nor storm can part
Me from His love so dear.

My Comforter

There is someone who walks with me
He knows each step I take.
I know that faithful He will be
He'll share in my heartaches.

Someone, who knows about my fears
He sees within my heart.
Through happiness and tears
I know He'll do His part.

He comforts me in times of need
As through this life I go.
He is my friend indeed
He knows my every woe.

This one whom I am speaking of
Is Jesus, Christ, God's Son
He died upon the cross for me
He is my precious one

My friend, He too will walk with you,
If you will only pray.
Confessing you're a sinner who
Needs His love today.

My Child

As the tears fell like drops of rain
God clearly spoke to me.
Child, I know you're upset
Those tears, my child, I see.

I know you do not understand
Why I'm leading in this way.
Child, you're finding it so hard
To accept my will today.

Trust me, my dear child.
Hold tightly to my hand.
It won't be long and I'll reveal
The blessing in my plan.

I love you, my dear child,
My grace through this you'll find.
Down life's road you will see
I had your best in mind.

My Big Easy Chair

I have a special place
To meet with God in prayer,
He speaks to me through His Word
In my big easy chair.

I wake up in the morning
Hurry to my easy chair.
I must not miss my meeting
With the Holy Spirit there.

In my big easy chair
I'll speak with God today.
He'll listen very patiently
To what I have to say.

Until the day He calls me home
Together we shall share.
Moments of sweet fellowship
In my big easy chair.

Mountain Top

When upon life's mountain top
Everything is going fine,
I'm feasting on the Manna
Of my Savior's love divine.

When upon life's mountain top
Soaring like a graceful dove,
Life's troubles seem so far away
While basking in God's love.

These mountain tops
Draw me from a world of care,
But while in the valley's darkness
I have learned the power of prayer.

You can be sure without a doubt
Life's valley's will appear.
God must remove the dross
Before the diamond is made clear.

Rather high upon the mountain top
Or in life's valley's far below,
God directs my footsteps
As along life's road I go.

A Mother's Love

A mother's love is truly sent,
From Heaven up above.
This world will never see
A stronger love.

A love that's freely given
With but one request.
Amid this troubled world
There will be happiness.

She doesn't mean to interfere
Get in her children's way,
But her love for them
Grows stronger everyday.

Sometimes she can be wrong
She's only human too.
The motives behind her actions
Are because of her love for you.

A mother's love is different
Explained it cannot be,
So very close to God's great love
I guess that's why it's free.

Missionary Mike

Missionary Mike came to our church
He's a pilot for the Lord.
Taking the Gospel to Indian tribes
Who have never heard God's Word.

I listened as he preached God's Word
Saw the burden in his eyes.
A pilot for my Lord,
He hears lost sinners' cries.

Missionary Mike made it clear,
Through him God clearly spoke.
Those lost souls need to hear
That Hell is not a joke.

I know that I'm not called to go
These tribes someone must reach.
So God will tell me what to give
So Pilot Mike can preach.

I Missed God's Blessing Yesterday

I missed God's blessing yesterday
When God spoke to my heart.
I should have listened to His voice
I should have done my part.

I missed God's blessing yesterday
I know He loves me still,
I cannot have His blessing
If I walk outside His will.

This blessing I will never know
Just what it held for me,
I missed God's blessing yesterday,
But now I clearly see.

To have God's blessings in my life
His will I must obey.
From now on you best believe
I'll let God have His way.

Man of God

A Man of God who preaches
What God would have him say,
Will surely find obstacles,
Placed within his way.

A preacher who seeks God's will,
To God this man is true.
A vessel that God can send
The Gospel message through.

Today it's hard to find
Preachers who take a stand,
Pleasing God their Savior,
Instead of pleasing man.

When one finally comes along,
It frightens Satan so,
That on this man of God,
He sends his every woe.

Satan will attack his health,
Send discouragement and despair.
Satan knows this man of God,
Is a man of prayer.

The Bible states resist the devil,
And he will surely flee.
Man of God, through faith and prayer,
You will have victory.

Made from the Hands of Man

In this world you will find
gods made of wood and stone.
If you want you can choose one
For your very own.

Made from the hands of man
With ears that do not hear.
Eyes that cannot see your needs
Nor even shed a tear.

These gods cannot utter words,
Nor stretch forth a loving hand.
A lifeless piece of nothing
Made from the hands of man.

I have good news to tell you
Now listen here to this,
In the Bible I have found
A real God does exists.

He came into this world
To set all sinners free.
Jesus Christ, God's only Son
Died on the cross for me.

Jesus arose from the grave
To claim me for His own.
I serve a living Savior
Not one that's made of stone.

Little Girls

Little girls are very different
In their personalities.
Some like fancy lacy dresses,
Some like faded dungarees.

Some like dressing up like Mommy
Playing dolls with company.
You'll also find that some of them
Will climb most any tree,

Little girls are full of giggles
Lots of hugs and kisses too.
God designed this little girl
Especially for you.

While thinking of your little girl
A young lady comes your way,
Dressed in her cap and gown
It's graduation day.

Life Is Like a Flower

Life is like a flower
Started from a tiny seed.
Planted deep within the earth
To serve the Planter's need.

From the seed that's planted
By the Planter's hand.
Blooms a pretty flower
To beautify His land.

Their fragrance tell the story
Of the Planter's special care.
His love for them is why
Their fragrance fills the air.

Then when the season's over
It is time to die.
Their petals drop one by one,
As they wave good-bye.

When we just like these flowers
From this world bid life adieu,
Will the Planter of our souls
Be as pleased with me and you?

Laughter

Many people go through life
Afraid to crack a smile.
Let me tell you, Christian friend
Laughter's not out of style.

Don't be afraid to laugh, my friend
I'm sure your face won't crack.
A merry heart's like medicine
That's a Bible fact.

God's children should not go around
With frowns upon their face.
I'm sure in Heaven's home on high
Frowns will be out of place.

So when you feel a good laugh
Coming up from deep within,
Remember in the Word of God
Laughter's not a sin.

In My Arms

Thank You for this baby, Lord,
You chose to send our way.
This tiny bundle in my arms
Will be a man someday.

Give us wisdom from above
Guide him along life's way.
Protect him from this sinful world
He'll have to face one day.

May our lives reflect your love
In us may he see you.
May the path we pave for him
Keep you in perfect view.

This bundle cradled in my arms
You've placed him in our care.
Help us to seek your will for him
Upon our knees in prayer.

In Grandma's Eyes

In Grandma's eyes I'm special
She loves me very much.
I see it in her smile,
And feel it in her touch.

In Grandma's eyes she sees
The very best in me.
I know my Grandma prays,
That someday great I'll be.

Grandma's eyes are filled with love
So gentle and so true.
I know this love is mine
Whatever I may do.

If I could paint a picture
Capture just where beauty lies,
On a canvas I would catch
The love in Grandma's eyes.

I Won't Be Disappointed

I won't be disappointed, Lord,
When things don't go my way.
I'll let you guide my footsteps
Through the moments of my day.

I won't be disappointed, Lord,
I'll place my trust in you.
Lord, you know the future
You know just what to do.

There is no need to panic
As life's trials come and go,
When I know my Savior
Is completely in control.

In times of disappointment
He's right there by my side.
So in the shadow of His wings
Is where I will abide.

I Need You

Lord, I need you
At the break of every day.
Before the sun has risen
And I am on my way.

I need to seek your presence
Cast on you my every care.
Satan's plans cannot prevail
When I seek your face in prayer.

I need You, precious Savior,
To protect me as I face
The events about to happen
As I move from place to place.

Then when my day has ended
I'm safely in my easy chair.
For your grace I need to thank you
As I end my day in prayer.

I Listened

As she spoke I listened
That's all that I could do.
I could feel the heartache
That she was going through.

She wondered why God allows
Heartaches, pain and strife.
They seem to overwhelm us
As we journey through this life.

As I listened I could hear
Her so softly cry.
I felt so very helpless
As I too wondered why.

God you know about her heartache
You know just what to do.
So I'll just do the listening
And leave the rest to you.

Goodbyes

Goodbyes are never easy,
But we will meet again.
The trip you're going on today
Is at life's journey's end.

Loved ones and friends so dear
Are waiting there for you.
Not so very long ago
They took this journey too.

You have walked along life's way
With Jesus hand in hand.
Now within His presence
Today you finally stand.

Leaving behind your footprints,
As you've traveled life's highway.
The trips we take to memory land
Will brighten our sad day.

Good and Bad

A question came to mind
As I began to pray,
Why do bad things happen
To good people every day?

Why do good people suffer
While oft times it's plain to see,
That the wicked seem to prosper?
This seems unfair to me.

My child, when it rains outside
It rains on one and all,
Sin touches good and bad
It has since Adam's fall.

No Fear

When I look around I am surprised
At what I hear and see.
God's children complaining, not seeking His will
In prayer upon their knees.

God's Word declares that wisdom begins
When the Lord we fear.
Down on our knees seeking and searching
Until His will is clear.

God's children have lost the joy
Of seeing God answer prayer.
No fear of God's chastening power
Wrapped up in worldly cares.

No fear of God almighty,
Who created the Universe.
Because in the life they are living
They do not put God first.

A Special Vessel

One day God shaped a vessel
Made it from a piece of clay.
Someday He would use this vessel
In a special way.

Within this special vessel
He placed His love divine.
A portion of His patience,
A tender heart so kind.

God filled her with His wisdom
Gently washed her face with tears.
This vessel God created,
Must be wise beyond her years.

A Mother, helper, and a friend,
To all who share her life.
God made a special vessel,
When He made a Pastor's wife.

A Miracle

I can expect a Miracle,
For by faith I stand.
Trusting Christ my Savior,
Who holds unto my hand.

He gave His life on Calvary,
To pay for all my sins.
His mercy opened Heaven's door;
And let this sinner in.

He sent His Holy Spirit
Who came to dwell within
The heart of this poor sinner
So a new life could begin.

New life in Christ my Savior
A Miracle indeed.
In faithfulness He supplies
Everything I need.

A Friend

Teach me, Lord, to be a friend
That is always kind and true.
A friend on whom one can depend,
A friend, my Lord, like you.

Teach me to be a friend who cares
For others round about.
A friend who always shares
A friend who will help out.

Teach me to be a friend who's near
Whenever there's a need.
A friend who sheds a tear;
When others don't succeed.

A friend who will not cause shame,
Nor grumble nor complain.
A friend who is the same
In either loss or gain.

A friend just like you are to me,
Christ Jesus from on high.
A friend like you I want to be
As each day passes by.

A Baby's Cry

She hears the faintest whimper
Of her baby down the hall,
Forsaking her much-needed sleep
She hastens to his call,

Her love is tightly wrapped within
That blanket lying there.
So thankful for this blessing
God has placed within her care.

She may not hear the traffic
Passing by her house at night.
Nor will she hear the hooting owl
Beneath the moon so bright.

You see, God gave her special ears
And you and I know why,
So she could sleep through anything
Except a baby's cry.

Wisdom

As I look back on my life
I'm filled with great remorse.
As a sailor on life's seas
Oft times I got off course

I see so clearly now that life
Is fading fast away.
But why was I so blind
In my younger days.

If only I could return
Retrace each step I took.
In this life one chance is all
You're given in life's book.

Once those years have passed away
No more to ever be.
With age comes all the wisdom
That youth could never see.

White unto Harvest

I've met a young couple
Sold out to the Lord.
They are leaving this country
Soon sailing abroad.

Fields white unto harvest
I heard them say,
Souls must be reached
Before judgement day.

Some missionaries travel
To lands far away,
While others labor in fields
Around them each day.

Whereever God calls them
To reap or to sow.
In fields white unto harvest
They are willing to go.

Until

Until you have walked the same pathway,
Your brother's walked in.
Until you have been tempted,
Enticed by the same sin.

Until you have felt the pain
Caused by your mistakes.
Cried the same tears,
Until your heart breaks.

Until God allows Satan
To sift you someday.
Your world crashes down
At your feet it does lay.

Until you have walked in his shoes
Do not judge him at all.
For in a moment of weakness
You also could fall.

Under Your Hat

Don't keep it under your hat
Hidden somewhere out of view.
Share the Gospel message
With a friend or two.

Looking back to the time
A few years ago,
When your heart was black with sin,
Because you didn't know.

Until someone cared enough
To share the Gospel story,
That Jesus Christ, God's only Son
Left His home in Glory.

The sinless, precious lamb of God
Allowed His blood to flow,
On a cross He paid sins price
He washed you white as snow.

Share the faith you now possess
Show the world that it is true.
There's not a hat that's big enough
To hide God's love from you.

Love's Dimension

It isn't hard to love
Those who love me in return.
But those who treat me unkind
To love them I must learn.

My flesh can love the lovable,
But that's not my intention.
Teach me, Lord, to love
Within true love's dimension.

I cannot love them on my own
For self gets in the way.
This earthen vessel must be filled
With Your love today.

To love the lovable
Is all that I can do,
When Your Spirit has control
I'll love the others too.

The One I Trust

Jesus is the One I trust,
As I walk along life's way.
Jesus is the One who guides me
He is my rock and stay.

Where would I be in this world
If I were traveling on my own?
There is no need for me to fret,
In this world I'm not alone.

I have met the Savior,
The one and only God.
I wait on His instructions
With His Word I'm shod.

I serve a living Savior
He holds me in His Hand.
God himself died on a cross
By faith in Him I stand.

The Next Backslider

The Bible states that backsliders
Will be filled with their own ways.
God chastens his children
When they go astray.

The man whom God chastens
Is a man who's truly blessed,
For the rod of God's correction
Is always for his best.

Who is a backslider?
Is there some way one can know?
Are there certain things they say?
Certain places where they go?

Yes, they are often known
By the things they say and do.
You can also find them sitting
In church upon a pew.

God tells us we must pray
Check our hearts each day anew.
If not the next backslider
Could very well be you.

The Bible

A man stood on a street
In a country far away.
Giving people Bibles
As they crossed his path that day.

The people took the Bibles,
A book in much demand.
This book they heard so much about
They now held in their hands.

I watched in such amazement,
As they begged the man for more.
As I looked I saw my Bible
On a table by the door.

Quickly I grasped my Bible
Fell upon my knees in prayer.
May I not take for granted,
What others find so rare.

The Best Time of My Day

The best time of my day
Is before the break of dawn,
When with God I fellowship
As we talk on and on.

Through His Word He talks with me
I speak with Him in prayer.
The best time of my day
Is this fellowship we share.

I bring to Him my burdens
Cast them at His precious feet.
Surrounded with His love
As we together meet.

In the early morning hours
I must not fail to keep
This meeting with my Savior,
While the world is fast asleep.

Start Anew

While walking down the road of life
You will stumble now and then,
Just pick yourself up off the ground
And start anew again.

It's not a sin to stumble
You see, all humans do.
Get up; shake the dust away,
God has a plan for you.

Victory lies just up ahead
In Christ the battle's won.
Get up; continue in the faith
Don't stop, you've just begun.

Forget mistakes made in the past
Press forward with a grin.
Faith will lift you to your feet
And grace will help you win.

A Soft-Spoken Man

The first time I saw Jesus
Was through a man of God.
A gentle, soft-spoken man
Who with God's Word was shod.

He did not speak to me with words
But in the most important way,
God revealed His love to me
Through this man's walk each day.

I saw the Lord's compassion on
This soft-spoken man's dear face.
Knew this vessel made of clay
Was the Spirit's dwelling place.

Watched Him face life's disappointments
Trusting in God's will divine.
While my faith in God did falter
His grew stronger all the time.

Lord, if you could teach me how to suffer
Yet by faith still stand.
I too would be Spirit-filled
Like this soft-spoken man.

Seek the Lord

Children, seek the Lord,
Hurry; don't delay.
Search for Him with all your heart
Let Him guide your day.

You will find a Lord who's near
Not a God who is afar.
The Lord is more than willing
To meet you where you are.

The Bible says draw near to God
And He'll draw near to you.
He's waiting with outstretched arms
That's all that He can do.

You'll find Him when you search for Him
With your whole heart in prayer.
That's when you'll have the power
To escape the tempter's snare.

Seasons

Have you ever walked along a beach
On a clear warm summer's day
And felt the heat of the sun
The Lord just sent your way?

As you watched the autumn leaves
Slowly falling to the ground,
Did you stop to thank the Lord
That autumn comes around?

In winter when the snow is white
As you watch the world at play,
Did you thank the Lord
For the snow He sent your way?

As summer turns to autumn
Autumn tells you winter's near,
Did you stop and thank the Lord
For the seasons of the year?

Promises

I have a book of promises
It's black and slightly worn
Once in a while I'll come across
A page that's slightly torn.

God's promises are written
In this book divine
I cherish every promise
In this book I find.

God promises eternal life
Through Jesus Christ, His Son
This book is full of promises
To each and every one.

This book reveals the future
Of things that soon will be
It promises that someday
Christ will return for me.

This book is the Holy Bible,
With God's love this book is bound,
In its precious pages
God's promises are found.

Piano

Piano, you're my special friend,
In a world so filled with cares.
A product of God's grace
Through answered prayer.

When I'm troubled and oppressed,
I touch your ivory keys.
The melody that comes from them
Puts my heart at ease.

You draw me from a world of care
Through melody and sound,
When praises to my Savior
At your ivory keys are found.

Piano, you bring pleasure,
The very thing I need.
A blessing from a gracious God
Is what you are indeed.

One Day

Have you ever seen a lion so fierce
Or watched a leopard stalking its prey?
In God's Word, the Bible states,
They shall become tame some day.

We will be able to hug a bear,
Or pet a lion along our way,
See a wolf and lamb romping around
Watch them busy at play.

The lion will eat straw like an ox,
The wolf and lamb together will dwell.
While a leopard will lay down with the kid
And a child will lead them as well.

These things will all come to pass
God promised them to be true,
Imagine hugging a bear or a lion,
While he cuddles up against you.

On a Shelf

In many homes across this land
The good old U.S.A.
The Bible sits and gathers dust
While God's children play.

They do not read God's Word
No time they have at all
In a corner sits their Bible
On a shelf against the wall.

If the truth were really known
Our hearts were opened wide
We'd see the reason from God's Word
His children run and hide.

The sin within their lives
Has caused this awful fall
That's why their Bible sits unread
On a shelf against the wall.

Omniscient, Omnipresent, Omnipotent

God works in wondrous ways
His wonders to perform.
He will guide my steps
Amid life's every storm.

I cannot see beyond
The moments of each day,
My God who is omniscient
He will guide my way.

When my world seems upside down
Storm clouds start to appear,
My God who is omnipresent
Whispers, child, I'm here.

God who keeps His promises
Will give me victory.
My God who is omnipotent
Fights life's storms for me.

Old Bible

I bought an old Bible
At a garage sale.
It was tattered and worn
But it told a tale

About the dear Christian
Long gone from this earth
Who dearly loved Jesus
For all she was worth.

I saw the tear stains
On the pages she read.
I knew this dear saint
By the Savior was led.

This precious dear saint,
Whose life's battles God fought
Were wrapped up in the pages
Of this Bible I bought.

A Child's Prayer

A little boy dressed in shabby clothes
Came to our church one day,
With unkempt hair and a dirty face
He began to pray.

Lord, I love you very much
You are so good and kind.
Thank you for always waking me
Just in the nick of time.

Mom and Dad love me too,
But Lord, they drink too much.
If they knew you like I do
They wouldn't need this crutch.

No one but you can understand
Just what I'm going through,
As I try to get myself
Off to Sunday School.

A Nobody

You may be a nobody
To the world all around
Of no value to the world
Just a nobody in town

A nobody watching while
The somebodies pass by
Why, they're much too busy
To stop and say hi

A nobody just wondering
Why they are on earth
Let me tell all the nobodies
What they're really worth.

You're worth the love of Jesus
'Twas for you and I
The King of Kings left Heaven's home
Upon the cross to die

A nobody you might be
To the world's point of view
Remember Jesus died to save
Nobodies just like you.

A Song's Memory

Each time I hear the song
"What A Day That Will Be"
I remember the friendship
That you shared with me.

I remember the times
We talked of our Lord,
The times we prayed
In one accord.

I was young in the Lord,
The Lord rightly knew
I had need of a friend
So He sent me you.

He gave you a voice
With a sweet melody,
How beautiful you sang
"What A Day That Will Be."

Someday soon that song
Will become reality,
God's trump will sound
Then Christ we shall see.

As for now, my friend,
I'll cherish the memory,
When I hear that old hymn
"What A Day That Will Be."

The Author of My Future

The present I can clearly see,
It's right before my eyes.
But by faith my future
With my Savior lies.

At times I find I wonder
What the future holds in store.
My Savior holds the key,
To the future's door.

As I look back on life
It is very plain to see.
Through each and every storm
My Savior went with me.

Like the author of a book
That has not been read,
My Savior knows each chapter
He knows what lies ahead.

Back Then

I couldn't understand back then,
When heartaches came my way
Why, Lord, you allowed Satan
To buffet me each day.

Back then I wondered
While I cried the whole night through,
How could you love me, Lord,
And allow the things you do?

Back then, my Lord, You understood
One thing I did not know.
These trials allowed in my life
I needed them to grow.

Back then amid those trials,
Seeds of faith began to grow.
It was your love and mercy
That allowed those tears to flow.

Bandages and Kisses

When you were just a tiny tot
And you fell and scraped your knee,
With tear-filled eyes I'd hear you say,
Mommy make it better, please.

I would cuddle you close to me
It seemed to heal your wound.
With just a bandage and a kiss
You would be smiling soon.

As the years passed swiftly by
Although I wished I could,
Mother's bandages and kisses
Didn't seem to do much good.

Now when your wounds are hurting
My heart is breaking too,
Instead of bandages and kisses,
In tears I pray for you.

I know the Lord will answer
Out of His love all mothers grew
With bandages and kisses,
God heals heartaches too.

Blessed with a Friend

Sometimes we go on shopping sprees
Shop the whole day through.
Together we bake cookies,
When there's nothing else to do.

We talk about our husbands
Only nice things do we say.
Of course we share recipes,
Make things like play dough clay.

Laugh as we make greeting cards,
For friends and family.
Out to lunch we must go
We need our energy.

One thing I am sure of
I'll bet my boots it's true,
Not many people have been blessed
With a friend like you.

Busy

Do you find yourself so busy
That you have no time to pray,
Asking God to guide you,
As you go about your day?

Are you so very busy
Running here and there,
Doing deeds of kindness
That you have no time to share,

The good news someone cared enough,
My friend, to share with you?
Now you find that you're too busy
To share the good news too.

Too busy doing temporal things
That soon will fade away.
Then, my friend, you are too busy
Throughout your walk each day.

Christian Home

I wasn't raised in a Christian home
Never heard my father pray,
Never heard him read God's Word
Wasn't raised in a Godly way.

I never went to church on Sunday
My mom never took me there.
I wasn't raised in a Christian home
Never knew the power of prayer.

I watched as sin destroyed
A family from within,
I wasn't raised in a Christian home
I lived in a world of sin.

When I had grown and married
I only knew one way,
So I walked in my parents' footsteps
Until I met Jesus one day.

He changed my life in an instant
This child who stood alone.
My friend, all of God's children
Weren't raised in a Christian home.

Daddy's Little Girl

It seems as if just yesterday
You sat on Daddy's knee,
Now here you are all grown up
A bride you soon will be.

You'll walk the aisle of your church,
With Daddy by your side
You'll hear the preacher say these words,
Who'll give away the bride?

A voice will speak so loud and clear,
Her Mother and I do,
You'll smile at that fine young man
Standing next to you.

As you speak wedding vows
You two will become one,
Daddy hasn't lost his little girl
Today he's gained a son.

Fiery Darts

When Satan's darts at you are hurled
Destruction is his goal.
Darts filled with heartaches and pain
Inflicted by the foe.

His fiery darts soar through the air
Leaving a trail of woe.
Satan robs, steals and kills,
The Bible tells us so.

Subtle in all his ways
Truly a bona fide liar.
To claim souls for his own
Is Satan's one desire.

Put on the shield of faith.
Satan's darts you soon will quench.
Armed with God's Word, the Spirit's Sword,
Victory will be a cinch.

With the Helmet of Salvation.
Surround yourself with prayer.
You will find God's peace amid
Those trials that you bear.

Five Minutes

I would say a little prayer
At the beginning of each day.
Why, I gave the Lord five minutes
Before I went my way.

I even read my Bible
Through in just one year.
Went to church one day a week
God's precious Word to hear.

One hour I would give the Lord
Thought Sunday morning was just fine,
I gave the Lord one hour
Of my precious time.

But there was something missing,
That from God I could not hide.
This ritual I was going through
Left me empty deep inside.

One day God's Spirit spoke to me
Child, this you must do,
With all your heart draw nigh to me,
And I'll draw nigh to you.

I sought my Lord with all my heart,
Found fellowship so sweet,
Now I can't spend enough time,
At my Savior's feet.

Golden Years

These golden years, so I've been told,
Are times of peace and rest
Golden years of sunshine
Life at its very best

A time when one retires
Sits back as time rolls by.
These golden years, so I've been told
Is a piece of apple pie.

Then why am I so worn out
With a body racked with pain.
My joints swollen and aching
Whenever there's a rain.

How come I can't remember
Where I put my teeth last night.
If I could find my glasses
They are probably right in sight.

Golden years, so I've been told,
Perhaps I misunderstood,
After all it's a fact,
I can't hear that good.

If by chance I've heard right,
These words were really spoken,
The one who told me such a thing
I'm sure must have been joking.

Grandchildren

I'm a grandma that's blessed,
Of this there's no doubt,
When my grandchildren
Run in with a shout.

They seem to appear
At just the right time,
When I'm feeling down
On my lap they will climb.

They give me a hug,
A few kisses too.
As they whisper, Grandma,
I love you,

They all are as different
As night is from day.
Lord, thank you for sending
Grandchildren my way.

Grandpa

Let me tell you about my grandpa
God made him just for me
There's not another like him,
For he's unique, you see.

Grandpa and I have lots of fun
You would never guess his age.
Grandma laughs and tells me
He's just going through a stage.

When God created grandpa
He used a special die.
For when he smiles,
There's a twinkle in his eye.

You could say that I am bragging
And perhaps that just might be.
I love my grandpa dearly
And I know that he loves me.

If Jesus Came to Your Church

If Jesus came to your church
I wonder what He'd say,
Would He see the love He taught us
Put to practice on that day?

Perhaps He'd come to your church
Dressed in garments worn and seedy.
Would He see hands stretched forth in love
To a stranger who is needy?

Or would He stand unnoticed,
Not knowing what to do.
While those who came in fine array
Are escorted to a pew?

God forbid that we should be
So thoughtless and unkind.
If Jesus came to your church,
I wonder what he'd find.

In God's Way

I cannot understand God's will
His will I must obey,
His voice spoke clearly to my heart
Child, you're in my way.

Your children trust in you,
To meet their needs each day,
I cannot deal with their hearts,
My child, you're in the way.

When they were small that was good,
Was then I worked through you
Now it is time that they must learn
To trust me as you do,

Now your work is complete,
It's time to let them go,
I've placed them where they are today
So in me they may grow

My child, your faith will increase, too,
In prayer you soon will say,
Thank You, Lord, for moving me
Out of my children's way.

If Only

Darling, if only you could learn
From all of my mistakes.
If only I could some way keep
You from the same heartaches.

If I could go ahead of you
As you travel life's highway.
I would remove from your path
The heartaches in each day.

If only what I've learned in life
Could be passed down to you,
If only my mistakes could teach
You a lesson too.

If only you could become
Wise beyond your years.
If I could only save you
From mistakes, I would, my dear.

If around you I could place a hedge,
Where heartaches dared not touch.
I would do it in a minute, dear,
I love you just that much.

In Touch

My daughter you're a woman now,
A little girl no more,
So beautiful in every way,
Much more than I asked for.

When I look at you, my dear,
This is what I often see
In the things you say and do,
I see a part of me.

I know that on some things in life
We find we disagree,
I'm glad we can communicate,
Express our thoughts so free,

But, my dear, I'm so in touch
With all of your hurts and fears,
When you're upset, my darling,
Your mother is in tears.

I know someday you'll understand,
You have a daughter too,
So be a little patient with
This mother who loves you.

Into This World

Lord, You know man's disappoints,
As he travels in this world,
You see as Satan angrily
His darts at man has hurled.

You know man's strengths and weaknesses,
As life's battles have been fought.
You know the pain and heartaches
As life's lessons have been taught.

You've watched with love so merciful
The wretchedness of sinful man,
To save his soul from hell
You had a perfect plan.

Into this world a King was born,
Lived as poor as man could be.
God Himself became flesh
To die for you and me.

Just Do the Right Thing

When you're up against a wall
Not knowing what to do,
The decision you're about to make
Will benefit just you.

Stop and think of your integrity,
Among friends and family.
The trust and respect,
The honesty they see.

Those benefits will bring a smile,
For a season bring some joy.
But what about those relationships
That soon they can destroy.

A little voice will whisper
In your ear so softly say,
Just do the right thing
And go merrily on your way.

Life Style

Life style evangelism does not work,
So I've heard it said.
If the Apostles lived today,
They would sadly shake their heads.

I'm sure they would not agree,
If they were alive today,
For one's life can tell a story,
Far more than words can say.

My friend, you are a Christian,
Christ died upon a cross for you,
Can your neighbors living near
Tell by the things you say and do?

Christ died for the all world,
They are watching you and me,
My Christian friend, your words
Must match the life they see.

When Life's Book Is Opened

When this flesh the Spirit dwells in
Is finally put to rest.
Will you stand before your Savior
Knowing you have done your best?

When the book is finally opened
Where your name is written down,
Will your love for Christ your Savior
By your works on earth be found?

Or will you stand before your Savior
Disappointed on that day,
Because you never took the time
To witness nor to pray.

The foundation that you build upon
Waits for you at Heaven's door,
Works that burn as hay and stubble,
Or precious stones shining forevermore.

Love of Money

The love of money rules man's life,
As through this world he trods.
Some love money to the point
That money is their god.
As I hold this money in my hand
These thoughts enter my mind.
In this piece of silver,
What feelings can I find?
It cannot buy me health
When I'm sick without a cure.
It cannot wash my sins away,
Before God makes me pure.
Money will not buy back youth,
When I'm old and gray.
Money will not bring me peace
On my dying day.
Money cannot buy God's love,
For it's a gift that's free.
Purchased by His only Son,
If heaven I'm to see.
When you leave this world,
What good will money do?
The money that you have,
You cannot take with you.
Perhaps that is why
I find its value small,
The important things in life,
It cannot buy at all.

Martha and Mary

Mary and Martha were sisters,
They walked with the Lord day by day,
Seeking their Savior's approval,
As they went along life's way.

Martha was ever so busy,
A worker, yes indeed.
Things were always so proper
When Martha took the lead.

Now Mary, she was quite different,
Too laid back, some people might say.
Martha would find Mary sitting
With Jesus just talking away.

This made Martha upset and quite angry,
Why is Mary just sitting there?
So Martha complained to the Master,
"Shouldn't Mary be doing her share?"

Jesus stated with love and compassion,
"Martha, you worry about many things;
What Mary is doing is needful
In the service of the King."

"The fields are white unto harvest
With much work to be done, I agree,
But how can my work be successful
If you forget about me?"

Mrs. Snow

I shall never forget the day,
Over forty years ago.
I went to church and sat beside
A lovely lady, Mrs. Snow.

As I sat and listened
I heard the Gospel story.
That Jesus Christ, God's only Son,
Left His home in glory.

The perfect Lamb of God,
For my sins His blood was shed.
Mrs. Snow quickly stepped aside,
As to the cross I fled.

I placed my faith in Jesus,
But without a doubt I know,
That day someone was praying,
Thank you, Mrs. Snow.

My Children Will Return

So often I hear people say
The Lord turned His back on them.
They were the ones who went astray,
And turned their backs on Him.

Once with the Lord they walked
In sunshine every day.
They thought their faith in Him was strong
Until troubles came their way.

The time had come for them to grow,
For they were standing still.
The Lord wanted them to know
How to walk within His will.

The Lord knew these trials had to be
Although it hurt Him so,
To see his children turn from Him
But He had to let them go.

He loves his children so He waits
Patiently for them to learn.
He has faith in them, you see,
His children will return.

Old Black Book

Since I have read this Old Black Book,
The Bible is its name,
Written by the hand of God,
My life is not the same.

In this Old Black Book
The message is quite clear,
That through the blood of Jesus
To God I can draw near.

God the Son came to earth
Bore my sins upon the cross,
To purchase my salvation
To redeem me from the lost.

Jesus Christ then arose,
From the grave so I could claim
Victory over sin and death,
Through His Holy Name.

I'm not ashamed of this Old Black Book
Nor will I ever be.
The Word contained in this Book
Has set this sinner free.

Old Farmhouse

An old farmhouse once stood
Among some old pines trees.
When winter winds would blow,
Sometimes we'd nearly freeze.

You see, it had so many rooms
We couldn't heat them all,
That old farmhouse on a hill
Among those trees so tall.

Winter brought on hard times,
But we were never sad.
We children were together
At home with Mom and Dad.

That old farmhouse is now torn down
But the memories linger yet,
When I pass those old pine trees
Where once that farmhouse sat.

One Door

Man can find many doors
By which to enter in.
But one door and only one
Can cleanse a man from sin.

Religion's door you will find
You're welcome to walk through
This door has stood for centuries
It's far from being new.

Then the door of righteousness
Is always open wide,
Where acts of righteousness are found,
Just on the other side.

Now we must not forget the door
Of good works along life's way,
Man thinks he is Heaven bound,
By the good he does each day.

But there's only one door to Heaven,
Jesus holds the key,
Man's sins were bought and paid for
On the cross of Calvary.

Pathway

Another year is past
Never more to be,
Once it was the future
Now it's history.

A place when for a while
This mortal soul did dwell,
A pathway down the road of life
Where teardrops freely fell.

At times I'd stumble to my knees
Then I'd feel the Savior's hand,
Lift me above the circumstance
And on my feet I'd stand.

Along this pathway many times
Laughter would fill the air,
As with my friends and family
Good times were never rare.

In this pathway most of all
God's faithfulness was found,
Amid the sad and happy times
God's blessings did abound.

Rapture

I'm looking for the rapture,
When Christ shall come for me.
The day will come when
God the Father I shall see,

Only the Father knows
Just when Christ will appear.
So I'll keep looking up
I know the time is near.

This is the blessed hope
For which I dearly yearn,
When Jesus left this world
He promised to return.

It is written in God's Word
The dead in Christ shall rise,
Then those alive in Christ shall be
Caught up to meet Him in the skies.

In the twinkling of an eye,
The trump of God shall sound,
All who belong to Jesus,
Homeward will be bound.

Real

You say that you love Jesus,
Whatever would you do
Without His gentle guidance
To face each day anew?

You say He's everything you need
In this world of woe,
Do you share with others
This Jesus that you know?

When you're around your friends
Do you so often find
The one who paid your sins great price
Is farthest from your mind?

Stop and think for just one moment,
How you, my friend, would feel,
If Jesus ignored your presence,
Would you think his love was real?

The Road Gets Rough

Lord, sometimes life's road gets rough
My steps so often fail.
I think I've had more than enough
As through this life I sail.

Then silently I come to
The throne of grace in prayer.
As I lift my eyes to you,
You ease my every care.

The day becomes bright as can be
New hopes enter my mind.
In your precious Word I see
A love so pure and kind.

You reassure me through your Word
Your comfort is so sweet.
The promises in your Word,
Make my day complete.

Rough as the road may be
You are my lifelong guide.
Beneath the shadow of your wings
Is where I'm going to hide.

Satan Trembles

Satan does not care, my friend,
About the good you do.
He doesn't care one single bit
If you keep the Golden Rule.

Go to church three times a week,
Satan does not care.
If you want to see him tremble,
Start spending time in prayer.

When Christians pray, Satan knows
That he is powerless.
To keep you from the throne of grace
He'll do his very best.

Don't neglect the house of God,
Good deeds with others share.
Just remember Satan trembles
When he sees a man in prayer.

Sons

Sons come in different colors
Shapes and sizes too,
A special gift from God
Especially for you.

He will fill your life with joy,
As you watch him grow.
It's at your feet that he will learn
The things that he should know.

He will watch each thing you do,
Listen to the words you say.
This little boy at your side
Will be a man someday.

God placed him in your care
He is your responsibility.
If you want a Christ-like son
Then Christ-like you must be.

Storm Clouds

I can see the storm clouds rising
Fierce as they may be,
I will not shudder at this storm,
My Lord, I'll trust in thee.

I cannot control the storm's strong winds
They will toss me to and fro,
My Savior, He will hold my hand
As through this storm I go.

It's not the first storm in my life
Nor will it be the last,
But as in storms of days before
My Lord will hold me fast.

Each storm cloud that arises,
To my Savior draws me nigh,
My faith grows that much stronger
With each storm that passes by.

Unity

If we would examine ourselves
Upon our knees in prayer,
Place our eyes upon the Lord
And keep them focused there,

Instead of criticizing one another
Let complaining not be found,
Then we would have God's blessings
As we climb to higher ground.

Praising God for showing mercy,
In His blessing we abound.
As we walk into God's house
Knowing we're on hallowed ground.

Then the message of the Gospel
Hindered it would never be.
If God's children want to please Him
They must walk in Unity.

Take a Chill Pill

In the morning when I wake up,
I see the rising sun,
I have this urge to hurry,
Many things I must get done.

My flesh hurriedly gets out of bed,
At the break of day,
Hurry up, let's get going,
My flesh will quickly say.

Don't take time to read your Bible,
You've already read it through,
Besides you can read it later,
There are more important things to do.

Flesh, you fight a losing battle,
The Bible is God's Holy Word,
I must seek my Lord's instruction,
Why are you being so absurd?

So flesh, just take a "Chill Pill,"
While I read God's Word and pray,
When our fellowship is over,
We'll be safely on our way.

Telephones

When telephones were invented,
What a glorious happy day.
We could keep in contact
With others far away,

What a blessing sent from God
To make life an easy road,
But man did not foresee
The dangers it could hold.

If telephones were used
For the purposes intended,
Instead of idle gossip
No one would be offended.

Satan saw a tool
To him it was so dandy,
How sad that there are Christians who
Help Satan make it handy.

The Savior Will Appear

In the twinkling of an eye,
The Savior will appear.
On this you can rely
The time is drawing near.

He will take us home to glory,
Ask us what we've done.
We will have to tell the story,
Of the souls that we have won.

How many have you told
The plan of my Salvation?
Our lives He will unfold
There will be no reservations.

So let us do our best
For Christ throughout each day,
So we can stand the test
When Jesus comes our way.

The Widow

A widow lady frail and weak
Held a mite in her hand.
She placed it in the offering plate,
Next to her stood a very rich man.

The rich man placed a large amount
In the offering plate that day.
While the widow lady frail and weak
Put in all of her pay.

The rich man had abundance left,
After the offering passed by.
He found it hard to part with his wealth,
While joy shone in the widow's eye.

The Lord told those standing around
This widow the world will recall,
For she gave abundantly,
The rich man gave nothing at all.

This Valley's Dark

This Valley's dark, Lord, I cried,
I cannot see beyond.
No matter, Lord, how hard I've tried
I cannot see the dawn.

This burden's growing heavier,
Lord, what will I do?
May your strength with me endure
To see this burden through.

I know you have a reason
To lead me in this way.
For just a little season
In this valley I must stay.

This valley's dark, but soon I'll see
You're precious will's bright glow.
From this burden be set free
And closer to you grow.

This Vessel

This vessel made of flesh and bone
So marred it was by sin,
This vessel looked outwardly clean
But God could see within.

The marks of sin were very clear
To God's almighty eye,
Although so very hidden
From others passing by.

Motives hidden deep within,
God saw them from the start.
Man only sees the outside,
God sees within the heart.

God took this meager vessel,
Just why I do not know,
Instead of casting it away
He washed it white as snow.

Throughout Eternity

When my Lord looks at me
I know He does not see
A sinner condemned to Hell
Throughout eternity.

My righteousness He does not see
The works that I have done.
He only sees the righteousness
Of Jesus Christ, His Son.

The Lamb of God who knew no sin,
His blood has set me free,
Abiding love that will last
Throughout eternity.

No longer bound by sin's strong hold,
Because of Calvary,
This sinner is saved by faith alone
Throughout eternity.

Sands of Time

I can't turn back the sands of time,
Start my life anew,
Go back to the blessed time
This sinner came to you.

Turn back the sands of time,
By faith just let you lead,
My Lord, I left your side,
Wasted years of sowing seed.

I can't turn back the sands of time,
Undo the things I did,
While outside of your perfect will
Under a bushel hid.

Hid from others all the joy
That Salvation brings,
Even hindered some lost soul
From knowing Christ my King.

The sands of time cannot recede,
But I can start from here,
May the life I live today
To thy cross draw others near.

Virtuous Women

As this woman crossed my path
I heard my Savior say,
A virtuous woman, my dear child,
Has just passed by your way.

This virtuous woman walks by faith
Along life's busy road,
Her price is far greater than
All of this world's gold.

As she spoke from God's Word,
Wisdom was her array,
The Holy Spirit filled the room
As she began to pray.

I'm so glad she crossed my path,
Lord, may I become someday
A virtuous woman just like the one
You just sent my way.

Walking in the Spirit

To walk within the Spirit's glow
Each moment of my day,
Where God's blessings flow,
And burdens ease away.

The Holy Spirit freely gives
Me peace within my soul,
For in my heart He lives
Through Him my life is whole.

When Jesus left this world of woe
The Spirit He did send,
How the blessings daily flow
As on Him I depend.

The Spirit gladly intercedes
In prayer before my King,
As He gently leads
With joy my heart can sing.

To walk within the Spirit's will,
This is my prayer today,
And let the Spirit daily fill
My life in every way.

Wedding Vows

Wedding vows were spoken
The two of you are one,
As man and wife your love will grow
The best is yet to come.

You'll laugh together joyfully,
Even shed a tear or two,
He'll be your knight in armor bright
You'll be his dream come true.

The love you feel this moment
Is small beyond compare,
To what you'll feel down the road,
As through the years you share.

The road that you have taken
Will have its ups and downs,
A marriage built upon God's love
Is built on solid ground.

Worry

The world calls me Worry
Misery's my middle name,
It's in the hearts of faithless men
I best can play my game.

You see that's what I bank upon
That way I never lose,
When looking for a partner
A faithless man I choose.

I'll shudder at a man of faith
With him I won't begin,
If faith is standing at his side
I can in no way win.

When faith is around you're sure to find
Worry nowhere in sight,
Worry quickly bites the dust
When faith gets in the fight.

Worship

I don't believe in shouting
Lord, how can this be?
These people seem so happy
But this shouting I can't see.

I can worship quietly, Lord,
I love You, there's no doubt,
But I'm too sophisticated
To ever loudly shout.

Then one day You spoke to me,
Saying, My children aren't the same,
Each one of them is different
As different as their names.

Some worship Me and shout
With a love so true,
Then some worship Me silently
The way you choose to do.

It's not the way they worship
That really counts, you see,
The condition of their heart
Reveals their love for me.

You Were There

Sometimes I've wondered could it be
My Lord is unaware
Of the struggles in my life
That fill me with despair.

In times of deep distress
Friends are seldom found,
Lord, you saw each tiny tear
That fell upon the ground.

In those times I could not see
My eyes were dimmed by tears,
It was your strength and grace
That led me through those years.

As I look back upon my life
I see your love and care,
Those times I thought I was alone
I now see you were there.

To order additional copies of

The GIFT of POETRY

Have your credit card ready and call:

1-877-421-READ (7323)

or please visit our web site at
www.pleasantword.com

Also available at: www.amazon.com

Printed in the United States
905600003B

9 781579 215316